ALEXANDER IN TROUBLE
and other stories

ACORN LIBRARY

LUCY M. BOSTON *The Castle of Yew*
KENNETH GRAHAME *The Reluctant Dragon*
MARGARET HAINSON *A Christmas Acorn*

NEW ACORN LIBRARY

EVA BEXELL *The Minister's Naughty Grandchildren*
GRISELDA GIFFORD *The Mystery of the Wooden Legs*
with HELEN CLARE *Seven White Pebbles*
GRISELDA GIFFORD *Ben's Expedition*
with PAMELA SYKES *Billy's Monster*
RENÉ GUILLOT *Pascal and the Lioness* with *Tipiti, the Robin*
WILLIAM MACKELLAR *Davie's Wee Dog*
with DAVID STEPHEN *Rory the Roebuck*
MARGARET POTTER *Tony's Special Place*
BETTY ROLAND *The Forbidden Bridge*
with *Jamie's Discovery*
CATHERINE STORR *Lucy*
with *Lucy Runs Away*

Alexander in Trouble
and other stories

SUSAN BURKE

Illustrated by Gavin Rowe

NEW ACORN LIBRARY
THE BODLEY HEAD
LONDON · SYDNEY · TORONTO

For the children at
Yaringa Primary School
and Willetton Special School,
Western Australia

British Library Cataloguing
in Publication Data
Burke, Susan
Alexander in trouble, and other stories.
(New acorn library).
I. Title II. Series
823'.9'1J   PZ7.B/
ISBN 0-370-30143-9

© Susan Burke 1979
Illustrations © The Bodley Head 1979
Printed in Great Britain for
The Bodley Head Ltd
9 Bow Street, London, WC2E 7AL
by BAS Printers Limited, Over Wallop, Hampshire
Set in Monophoto Plantin
First published 1979

CONTENTS

Alexander Has a Birthday, 7
Alexander in Trouble, 12
Alexander Makes a Cake, 22
Alexander Gets Bogged, 31
Alexander and William Tell, 42
Alexander in the Bath, 53

Alexander Has a Birthday

Alexander Jones was up early to open his birthday presents. At school that day everyone sang 'Happy Birthday', and after school his friends gave him a 'Birthday Push' home. Alexander usually insisted on wheeling his chair himself, but this was a special day, and it was great fun. As they raced past the corner shop, Mrs Bracken the shopkeeper looked out and called,

'Hi, Alexander. Stop!'

The children pulled at the chair to slow it down.

'Reverse!' shouted one boy.

'Stop!' screeched one of the girls.

'About turn!' ordered someone else.

Jostling and puffing, they turned back. Mrs Bracken smiled at Alexander.

'Today's your birthday, isn't it? Happy Birthday!' And she handed him a parcel.

'Thank you very much,' said Alexander. 'How did you know it was my birthday?' But Mrs Bracken had disappeared inside her shop.

'Come on—let's go and open my present in the

park.' Alexander had hardly finished speaking before his friends grabbed the wheelchair and they all set off again. When they reached the park, Alexander had to hang on tightly to both his chair and his parcel as they bumped over the grass. The others flopped to the ground panting.

'I think I'll push myself home, thanks,' said Alexander. Then he opened his parcel, and everyone crowded round to look.

Inside the paper was a shiny white box, tied with a blue ribbon, and with 'Fine Chocolates' printed on it in silver letters. As Alexander lifted the lid a delicious warm brown smell floated out. Rows of fat chocolates sat snugly in their paper nests. Some were round and some were square. Some had dimples, and others had nuts on top. One or two had icing squiggles and a couple were wrapped in gold and silver paper. What a present! Inside the lid was a picture which showed what was inside the chocolates—pineapple cream, Turkish delight, toffee, peppermint, strawberry jelly and almonds. Mouth-watering!

Alexander knew everyone was longing for a chocolate, and he handed the box to Lucy.

'Pass them around for me, will you, please?'

'Only one each,' Lucy warned.

'Thanks, Alexander.'

'Are you sure?'

'Gosh, if they were mine, I'd hide them under my bed!'

'Mmm. Thanks a lot.'

'This one with the gold paper looks good.'

Alexander began to feel uneasy. Perhaps there wouldn't be any chocolates left for him?

After everyone had had their choice, Lucy gave the box back. Alexander put the lid on quickly.

'We'd better get going,' he said. 'But this time please keep all the wheels on the ground!'

At Alexander's gate, they gave him one last shove.

'Goodbye!'

'Goodbye!'

'Thanks for the chocolates.'

Just then Alexander's mother came round the side of the house.

'Hallo, dear,' she said. 'Did I hear the magic word "chocolates"?'

Alexander told her about Mrs Bracken's present. 'How did she know it was my birthday?' he asked.

'Oh, I told her when I bought the candles for

your cake,' smiled Mrs Jones. 'Let's see these famous chocolates. It was very kind of Mrs Bracken, wasn't it?'

Alexander opened the box—and stared. There were only two left! He handed them quickly to his mother.

'There's one for you,' he said shakily, 'and one for Dad—and that's all.'

'Al-ex-*ander*!' gasped his mother. 'Don't tell me you've eaten all the others already—you'll be sick!'

Alexander blinked to keep the tears of disappointment from his eyes. 'I gave the others away. I haven't had any myself!'

Mrs Jones took the box and put back the two chocolates. 'Well, then,' she said, 'you must have the two that are left. Dad and I won't mind.'

Alexander blew his nose. Was it awful of him to wish now that he hadn't given away all the other chocolates?

As Mrs Jones was handing the box back she suddenly stopped. Then she shook it, and with a grin, lifted some of the paper out. There, underneath, were a whole lot of chocolates sitting snugly in their paper nests. Some were round and some were square. Some had dimples, and others had nuts on top. One or two had icing squiggles and a couple were wrapped in gold and silver paper.

'How on earth did they get there?' asked Alexander.

His mother laughed. 'The box has two layers,' she explained. 'The top layer has all been eaten, but there are more chocolates underneath.'

Alexander made a face. 'Just think, I might have

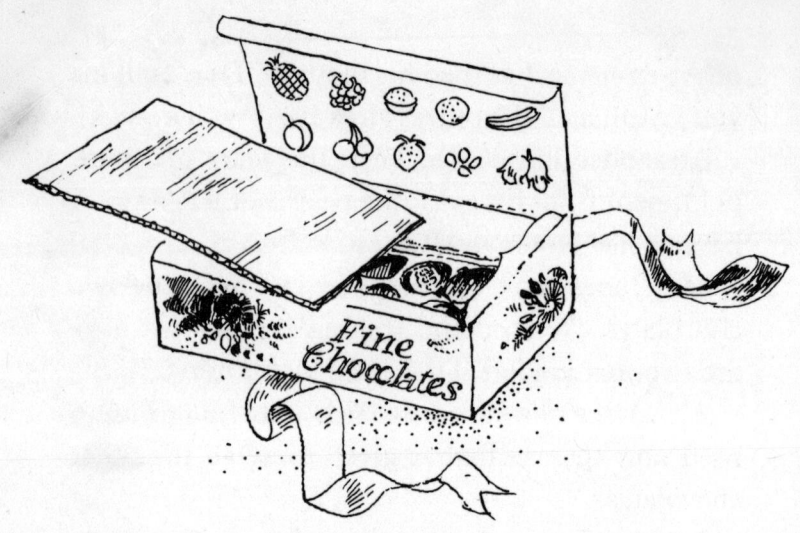

thrown the box away, thinking it was empty.'

His mother gave his hair a friendly tug. 'Come and put the candles on your birthday cake,' she said.

So he did.

Alexander in Trouble

One cold Saturday morning Alexander was in the park playing with his friends. Tony had brought a ball and they were throwing it quickly, one to the other, faster and faster. Anyone who dropped it was out. Alexander was good at catching; he had strong arms and could throw hard. One by one they dropped out until only Alexander and three others were left in the circle. Just then there was a rumbling sound in the air. It became steadily louder.

'Stop a minute!' said Tony.

They listened, and the rumble became a growling, the growling became a chugging, the chugging grew louder and turned into a roar—and down the road swept a crowd of policemen on magnificent black and white motorbikes. Rows of dark uniforms and shiny white helmets moved down the middle of the road like one huge machine. The noise was so tremendous that the children had to shout to make themselves heard.

'Wow!'

'Look at those fantastic motorbikes!'

'What are they doing?'

'It's a parade—for the Police Exhibition this afternoon.'

'Where?'

'At the Showground.'

The noise faded as the bikes swept past and disappeared over the hill.

'I'm going to ask my Mum to take me to see them,' announced Lucy, skipping up and down.

Alexander agreed. 'I'll ask my Mum, too.'

'My sister's got German measles,' said Bridget moodily, 'so I bet we don't go.'

'Weren't those bikes great?' said Tony, wonderingly.

'My brother has a motorbike just like those,' piped up Giuseppe, the smallest of them all.

'My big sister has a bright red motorbike,' boasted Anna.

'And *my* little sister has bright red spots ...' Bridget tried again, but no one was interested.

Tony threw some grass at Anna. 'Go on, Anna—your sister's only got a scooter.'

'Well, I wouldn't mind only a scooter,' complained Alexander, 'or even an ordinary bike like yours.'

'Well now. Listen to him!' shrugged Bridget. 'You've got two beautiful big wheels already!'

Alexander turned to look at her. 'Okay, then, Bridget. I'd like to see you try my wheels.'

'Oh, I bet it's easier than riding a bike,' replied Bridget airily.

Alexander was annoyed. 'All right, smarty,' he said. 'I'll get out and you can sit here, and then we'll see just how good you are.'

Alexander could get out of his chair quite easily by himself if there was something beside it to sit on, but he was too impatient to waste time finding a park bench. So he called, 'The crane, Lucy.'

Lucy laughed as she and the rest of the 'crane' went to lift him. They had done it plenty of times and were pretty good. Lucy and Andrew took Alexander's elbows, while Fred and Giuseppe supported his knees.

'One, two, three, lift!' commanded Lucy, and in three seconds Alexander was sitting on the ground.

'In you get, Bridget.'

Bridget hopped into the chair and held the handrails. Alexander stopped feeling cross and tried not to laugh as Bridget tugged the wrong way and the chair went backwards. Bridget blushed and tried again. This time she moved forwards, but it was much harder than she had expected and turning round took a lot of pulling and pushing. Before long her shoulders began to ache, and her arms were getting tired.

'It's worse than rowing a boat!' she panted at last.

'Of course, it's easier on the footpath,' Alexander relented, 'and your arms don't get tired when you're used to it.'

Bridget had got the chair moving slowly forwards and then back again. 'Can I ride down to the lily pond?' she asked. 'I'm getting the hang of it now.'

'All right,' agreed Alexander, 'but hurry up. The ground feels freezing.'

'Okay, I'll be quick,' Bridget promised. 'Just watch me.'

Eager to show how fast she had learned to work the chair, Bridget pushed really hard at the handrails. Her steering was pretty wobbly but she was soon moving very quickly over the slippery grass. Behind her the others cheered.

'Move!'

'Faster, slowcoach!'

'Hope you know how to stop!'

Bridget was getting closer and closer to the pond. Too close—and too fast! She grabbed at the handrails, but they slid through her cold fingers. She could hear the children shouting.

'Stop, Bridget. Look out! Put on the brakes!'

'I *CAN'T*,' she wailed.

The wheelchair hit a bump and lurched to one side. Bridget screamed and stood up. The chair overbalanced, Bridget went flat on her face and the chair cartwheeled neatly over her and into the pond,

SPLOSH!

While the others raced to help her, Lucy stayed with Alexander who was looking a bit scared. 'Now look what's happened. I should never have let her try out my chair.'

Lucy frowned. 'She certainly could have been more careful—but don't worry. I'm sure she's not badly hurt. Just as well she didn't land in the pond too.'

The others came back slowly with poor Bridget. Her face and hands were scratched, and her legs were bleeding. She was crying, and Alexander felt guilty.

'Gosh, I'm sorry, Bridget,' he said. 'Are you hurt much?'

Bridget wiped her eyes with the back of her hand, leaving a grey streak on her face. 'I don't care about that,' she sniffed, 'but I've wrecked your wheelchair!' and she burst into fresh tears.

Lucy gave her a quick hug. 'It'll be all right, Bridget.'

'I'm afraid we can't fish the chair out without half-drowning ourselves,' announced Fred, 'so Anna has gone to fetch Alexander's father to help.'

'I bet he'll be furious,' said Alexander.

This made Bridget cry even louder.

'That was a dumb thing to say,' Andrew whispered to Alexander. 'Now you've made her feel even worse.'

Alexander shrugged his shoulders. He felt pretty bad himself. Lucy asked if anyone had a clean hanky. Giuseppe had the cleanest, so Lucy wet it under the nearest tap and began to mop some of the dirt off Bridget.

When Anna arrived with Mr Jones, the children looked at him apprehensively, hoping he wouldn't be too cross. But Mr Jones could see that everyone was miserable enough already.

'Okay, kids, let's get this sorted out,' he said. 'Andrew and Tony, will you give me a hand?'

It wasn't long before the wheelchair was hauled out of the pond and safely folded away in Mr Jones' car. Mr Jones drove Bridget home first and explained about the accident, then he took Alexander home, where his mother was waiting. Alexander was given a lecture on carelessness and sent to bed.

'Well, this is a mean sort of punishment,' he thought, and he gave a gigantic sneeze.

The bedroom door opened and his mother looked in.

'Aachoo!' exploded Alexander again.

Mrs Jones nodded. 'I knew you'd catch a cold after sitting around on that damp ground in the park, which is why I put you straight to bed.'

She gave him a hanky, just in time for the next sneeze. Alexander blew his nose and protested, 'But colds come from germs, Mum.'

Mrs Jones ignored him. 'Dad has taken your chair to be mended and it will take a week to fix that twisted wheel.'

'Oh, no!' Alexander felt very gloomy. 'What will I do without it?'

'Perhaps you'll stay out of trouble,' suggested his mother as she closed the door.

But Alexander hardly missed his chair after all. His cold turned out to be German measles, so he was in bed for the next week anyway.

And, by the way, although he didn't really deserve it, Alexander managed to see the parade at the Police Exhibition. He saw it two days later—on television!

Alexander Makes a Cake

'Wake up, Alexander!' Mrs Jones went to the cupboard and took out his clothes. 'It's already half-past nine, and I must go shopping.'

Alexander rubbed his eyes and yawned. 'Why do I have to get up just because you're going shopping?'

'No need to be rude,' said his mother, pulling back the blankets. 'Dad's out, so I'm the only one to help you—unless you want to sit around in pyjamas all day.'

Alexander tried to pull back his blankets. 'Can't I just finish my dream?'

'No,' said his mother, hurrying off his pyjamas and hustling on his underpants and trousers. Someone had to do this because Alexander couldn't move his legs, but he always put on his other clothes himself. He slid into his wheelchair to get out of the way while his mother made the bed.

'Have you forgotten that Mrs Pritchard is coming for lunch?' said Mrs Jones, tucking in the blankets. 'I must get to the supermarket and have the house tidy by twelve o'clock.'

Alexander struggled into his T-shirt. 'Do you want me to help?'

'Yes, please, dear,' said his mother, as she gave the pillows a final thump. 'I'd like you to dry the dishes after you've had your breakfast and then set the dining room table. I've left everything ready.'

'Okay,' said Alexander. 'So long as you don't want me to make a cake or something.'

Mrs Jones tied his shoes. 'That would be lovely too, dear, but there's no time to worry about that. Now I must rush.'

She gave him a hurried kiss, which landed in his eye, and dashed off.

Alexander was wiping the kiss out of his eye when he had a brilliant idea. He would make a cake! It would be a terrific surprise for his mother. There wasn't much time, but if he made the cake first, he could do everything else while it cooked. He forgot about brushing his hair and washing though he did remember to eat his breakfast. He found his mother's cook book and looked up *CAKES*. One recipe had a tick by it, and looked quite easy.

'Beat 4 eggs and 1 cup sugar until light. Add 1 cup self-raising flour, and lemon essence. Bake at 200° C for 15 minutes.'

Alexander knew that the oven must heat up and he whizzed over to turn it on. Oh, no! He couldn't reach the knob. Back to the other side of the room and he scrabbled around in a couple of drawers until he found the long salad tongs.

'Gosh, I'm clever,' he boasted, wheeling himself back to the stove. Very carefully, he leant over and used the tongs to turn the oven knob. Then he went to the 'fridge.

'Four eggs,' he remembered, 'and the butter to grease the cake tin.'

He found the butter without much trouble but the eggs were just a bit too high for him to reach comfortably. One egg, two eggs, three eggs—then *SPLAT*. Alexander looked at the smashed egg on the floor. Bother, it was the last one and he couldn't get down to clean it up, so it would just have to stay there. He shut the 'fridge door. 'Oh, well,' he said hopefully, 'I'll have to make do with only three eggs.'

Everything went quite well until Alexander came to the lemon essence part. The recipe didn't say how much to use. He looked at the label on the little bottle.

'Two or three drops. Drops? That can't be right.

How could anyone taste a few tiny drops in a whole cake?'

He thought for a moment, and then decided. 'It must mean two or three teaspoonfuls.'

So in went three teaspoonfuls of lemon essence!

The cake was ready for the oven. Alexander set the timer with the salad tongs. 'Fifteen minutes exactly—now in goes the cake.' He was very pleased with himself.

He put the dirty dishes in the sink, but he couldn't reach down far enough to put the plug in so he couldn't wash them. He began to wipe the dishes his mother had left on the draining board. Before long, Alexander could smell his cake cooking—a warm, lemony smell. Delicious! He looked at the clock. Oh dear, five to eleven and his mother would be home soon. He hurried into the dining room to set the table. Just as he was struggling with the tablecloth he heard a 'ping' from the oven timer. That meant the cake was done. He threw the tablecloth into a chair and raced back to the kitchen.

'Where's the oven glove? Oh, bother, on the floor. I'll have to use a tea towel.'

Getting the cake out of the oven wasn't easy. First he burnt his fingers, and then he nearly dropped the tin, but at last it was safely on the table. He took another look at the clock. Quick! Ten past eleven, and the table wasn't set.

It took Alexander a long time to lay the table. The tablecloth kept slipping, and the more he tried to hurry, the more he fumbled. He had almost finished when he dropped a whole bunch of spoons on the floor.

'Too bad,' he sighed, 'but at least the rest is done.'

Half-past eleven. How awful if Mrs Pritchard arrived before his mother got back. Mrs Pritchard was a very fussy person, and Alexander could just imagine the look on her face when she saw the egg on the kitchen floor, and the spoons all over the dining room. Just then, Mrs Jones opened the front door.

'Oh, the traffic,' she complained, dumping the grocery bag on the floor. 'It took ages to park the car and the supermarket was just crammed with people.'

'Hi, Mum—come and see what I've done!'

First his mother looked in the dining room.

'Good boy,' she said, picking up the spoons at her feet. Then they went into the kitchen. 'Thank you for doing the dishes,' she stopped. 'Oh, how did that egg get on the floor?'

'Well, I dropped it while I . . .' began Alexander, but his mother interrupted. She had seen his cake.

'Alexander—how marvellous!' She turned the cake out of the tin and weighed it in her hand. 'Quite light. You *are* a clever boy.' She smelt it 'Smells good, too.' She sniffed again. 'Actually—it's extremely lemony,' she said, looking puzzled. 'Do you mind if I have a tiny taste?'

She cut a thin slice from the side of the cake, and took a bite. Her face had a very peculiar look. Alexander felt his heart sink.

'What's the matter?' he asked anxiously.

Mrs Jones tried to smile. 'How much lemon essence did you use?'

Alexander answered slowly. 'The cook book didn't say, so I put in three teaspoonfuls.'

'Oh dear!' said his mother. 'You only needed a few drops. Have a taste.'

Alexander tried the piece of cake, and he made a face. The lemon taste was much too strong. No one would want to eat it. His lovely surprise was wasted.

'I think I'll read a book for a while,' he said in a chokey voice.

'Oh, no you don't,' said his mother, spinning his chair round. 'You stay right here.'

She took some cream from the 'fridge and handed him the beater. 'Now, whip that for me, please.'

Mrs Jones sliced up the warm cake and put the pieces into a glass bowl. As Alexander began to beat the cream, he wondered what was going to happen next. Out from the 'fridge came a custard carton. Glop, glop, went the custard over the cake. Mrs Jones took the whipped cream from Alexander and spread it over the custard, then she smiled.

'Nearly finished.'

After a quick look in the cupboard she found a packet of cherries to decorate the top.

'Good!' she said, and began to clean the smashed egg off the floor. 'You had better wash that cream off your face,' she said to Alexander, who was busy licking the beater. 'Mrs Pritchard will be here soon!'

A couple of hours later, Mrs Pritchard put down her dessert spoon with a little sigh.

'Well, my dear,' she said to Mrs Jones, 'that certainly was the most delicious trifle! You simply must let me have the recipe.'

Mrs Jones looked across the table at Alexander and winked.

'Oh, I'm afraid that's a family secret,' she said.

Alexander Gets Bogged

Alexander scowled at his untidy desk. He picked up the model plane he was making and scowled at the tail.

Mr Jones glanced at him over the top of his newspaper. 'What a dreadful face!' he remarked.

Alexander scowled at him, too. 'This is a stupid plane,' he muttered.

'Looks all right to me,' Mr Jones said. 'What's stupid about it?'

Alexander sighed. 'This piece of wood is supposed to go in the slot. Well, it doesn't, and nothing else fits either.'

'No wonder,' said his father as he fitted the wood neatly in the slot. 'You were trying to put it in sideways.'

'Too bad,' grumbled Alexander ungratefully. 'I'm sick of it anyway.' He propped his chin on his hands and gloomily watched the rain outside pelting against the windowpane.

Mr Jones put the plane back on the desk. 'What's the matter with you today? You've been grizzling all morning.'

Alexander said miserably, 'I'm tired of sitting inside all day long. What's the use of holidays when you can't go out and play?'

Mr Jones picked up his newspaper. 'Complaining won't change the weather,' he said.

'Other kids play in the rain,' sulked Alexander.

His father grew impatient. 'Alexander, I want to get outside to finish the gardening, but I can't because of the rain. And since I'm stuck inside I would like to finish making Mum's new bookcase, but I can't because the hammer has disappeared. I've looked everywhere for it but it must have grown legs and walked away. I'm just as bored as you are.'

Alexander began to bite his fingernails. 'I hang around this house so much they call me, "Alexandy-Mummy's Handy",' he growled.

Mr Jones folded his paper. 'Stop chewing your nails, and let's have a game of Scrabble,' he said. 'When the rain stops you can help me in the garden.'

To everyone's relief after lunch the weather cleared up. Alexander and his father left the half-finished game and went out into the back garden. Mr Jones' black rubber boots squelched as he walked down to the little tool shed. Alexander waited impatiently as he clumped back with a spade, a fork and the hedge-trimming shears.

'I'm going to finish digging the vegetable patch,' said Mr Jones.

'What about me?' asked Alexander.

Mr Jones took some string from his pocket. 'You can clip the hedge.' He tied one end of the string to the shears and the other to Alexander's belt. 'There you are. If you drop the shears, pull them back with the string.'

Alexander opened and shut the shears excitedly. 'Thanks, Dad!'

'It will be hard work,' his father warned. 'Just clip as far as you can reach, and I can finish the tall bits later.'

At first Alexander attacked the hedge at top speed, but pretty soon he found that it was indeed hard work. He slowed down to a steady pace and concentrated on trimming the hedge as evenly as he could. The branches dripped water all over him, his hands grew cold and numb, and wet leaves stuck to his face. A couple of times he dropped the shears and had to pull them back with the string. At last his father called to him.

'Let's go and have tea!'

Alexander stopped thankfully and stretched his aching shoulders. He looked at his father and laughed.

'You're covered in mud!'

Mr Jones grinned through the mud on his face, and wiped his muddy hands on his muddy trousers. 'There's nothing like good clean mud.' He looked at the hedge. 'That's a good bit of work you've been doing. You've saved me all the back-breaking bits.'

Alexander felt very proud.

After they had eaten a huge tea, Mr Jones got to his feet. 'Well, I've finished the digging, and after I've washed this mud off, I'm going to buy some seedlings. Do you want to come with me?'

Alexander looked at the hedge. There was not much left to do.

'No, thanks,' he answered. 'I'm going to finish the hedge.'

'Are you sure?' asked his father. 'I'm dropping Mum off at the Library on the way, so you'll be alone for a while.'

'I don't mind,' said Alexander.

When his parents had gone, he set to work again and before long he had finished. He looked about the garden, and decided that since he had got the hang of it, he might as well begin clipping the hedge on the other side of the garden too. How surprised his father would be! Slowly he wheeled down the narrow path beside the muddy vegetable patch. The path would have been firm enough in dry weather, but the rain had made it soggy, and Alexander was only halfway across when the damp earth at the edge of the path crumbled.

'Oh, no!' He immediately pulled his chair backwards but it was too late. One big wheel had slipped and sunk into the soft, newly dug soil. In despair Alexander pulled and tugged at the wheel, but it only sank further in until the wheelchair was leaning dangerously to one side. He tried moving the wheel which was still on the path. No good.

'What can I do?' he thought frantically. 'I'm going to fall out!' The wheelchair, already leaning sideways, began to tip forward. The shears hit the footrest as they fell from Alexander's lap, and he gave a final desperate yank on the wheel as he slid helplessly out of the seat.

He lay on the muddy ground for a minute, squeezing his eyelids against tears of anger and frustration. Then he drew a deep breath and opened his eyes. He was lying on his face with one foot stuck between the footrest and the wheel of the chair, but he was not hurt. The shears lay beside him. He untied them and threw them on to the path so they wouldn't get lost in the mud. Now, what was he going to do? He was just thinking, 'I can't lie here in the mud till Mum and Dad get home,' when a big wet drop splashed on his hand, and then another.

He looked up at the sky. 'That's all I need. Now it's going to pour!'

The sun was already disappearing behind dark clouds, and the house seemed to be an awfully long way away. It looked as though he'd be half-drowned by the time his parents came back. Alexander glanced round—of course! The tool shed! It was only just across the vegetable patch and much closer to him than the house. Then he remembered that one foot was stuck in the chair. He wriggled around and clutched hold of his shoe, and after a bit of jiggling managed to tug it free. It was raining harder now and he was beginning to get very wet.

Alexander tried to struggle across the muddy ground. Usually he got around pretty well without his chair by sitting up and sort of rowing himself backwards with his arms, but the ground here was so slushy he couldn't even roll off his stomach. He had to try something else. At first he tried dragging himself over the soft soil as if he was swimming. After a bit he realised that he wasn't getting anywhere, so he tried rolling again and that was no good either. He was soaking wet by now and smothered in mud. Rivers of water ran down his face into his eyes and nose and mouth, making him blink and splutter. He flicked his wet hair out of his eyes, and then he had another idea. This time it worked. He began to walk on his elbows, wriggling from side to side like a worm, with his legs dragging behind him. That was much better—except that it nearly dragged his trousers off and his shirt began to fill up with mud. If only it wasn't pouring so and now the sky was getting quite dark. Alexander kept going doggedly. He had a crick in his neck from holding his face up out of the mud. Oh well, at least he was moving slowly and surely towards the tool shed.

'Nearly there!' he panted.

In a funny sort of way he was rather enjoying his muddy struggle. It was quite exciting to be quite deliberately grovelling in the dirt and slush. Alexander grinned as he thought with satisfaction that he'd never been so utterly filthy or thoroughly plastered with mud in his life.

Crack!-Boom! Thunder! His grin faded, and Alexander wriggled along faster. He didn't much like thunder. Finally, with one last heave, he was inside the shed. It was dusty and dark, and smelt of fertiliser and old sacks, but Alexander didn't care. He was glad to be out of the rain, which was now coming down by the bucketful. His wet clothes stuck to his skin, cold and clammy. He began to shiver. He looked round the gloomy little shed and wondered if there was an old raincoat or something he could wrap round himself and then he saw the heaps of sacks. Just the thing to keep him warm! He wriggled on top of them and pulled a couple over himself. They smelt awful, and he hoped there were no spiders in them. He tucked his cold legs under the rough sacks, propped his head on a bag of peat moss, and slowly he began to feel warm again.

Bother! Something hard was sticking into his shoulder. Alexander shifted his position a bit, but it was still there. Too bad, he wasn't going to move again now. He closed his eyes and listened almost happily to the rain drumming on the roof. He forgot the smell and the spiders. He even forgot the thing that was bruising his shoulder. Soon he drifted off to sleep.

'There he is!'
Alexander blinked his eyes in the glare of the torchlight on his face. His father and mother were back.
'Oh, Alexander!' To his surprise his mother

began to cry. She put her arms round him and squeezed him tightly. 'We couldn't find you anywhere in the house. And then we found your chair stuck on its side in the mud . . .'

Mr Jones patted her shoulder. 'Everything's all right now, dear.' He knelt down beside Alexander, who was rubbing his sore shoulder and feeling under the sacks for the offending object.

'I'll carry you back to the house,' said Mr Jones. 'You had us worried for a bit.'

Mrs Jones swallowed back her tears. 'How on earth did you get in here? And what happened?'

'Let's get him inside first,' Mr Jones said. 'Alexander can explain later.'

As Alexander sat up, his mother saw the mud caked on his clothes, plastered in his hair, and smeared all over his face and arms. 'Oh!' she gasped, ready to burst into tears again.

Alexander smiled as his fingers closed over the hard thing that he had been sleeping on.

'It's all right, Mum. It's only good clean mud. And what's more,' he brandished his find triumphantly, 'I've found the hammer!'

Alexander and William Tell

Alexander enjoyed staying with his uncle and aunt. They had an enormous rambling garden which was big enough to get lost in. There were bookcases full of old and interesting books to read, sometimes Aunt Rosemary taught him complicated card games, and he could help Uncle Bernard in his garage workshop. There was always plenty to do. The morning after Alexander arrived for a holiday, Aunt Rosemary announced:

'There's a new family moved in next door with a boy about your age. Perhaps you could make friends with him. I think his name's Willy, or something.'

After breakfast, Alexander took his book into the garden. He sat for a while, feeling the sun on his face and the breeze in his hair. It was a lovely place. There were so many bushes and trees that the house was almost hidden. Uncle Bernard had once planted flowers here and there beside the winding brick path, but he had forgotten about them soon after, so only a few straggly ones remained.

A long way down the garden a small group of fruit trees stood on a patch of wispy grass. The path ended there and the rest of the big garden was more like a jungle. Alexander longed to explore, but it was too thick for him to crawl around in—he needed a bit more room when he was grounded. He took his wheelchair as far as the path went, and stopped by the trees in a patch of sunlight. He tried to read, but he just couldn't concentrate. At last he closed his book and just sat dreaming. Suddenly he heard a rustling in the bushes. Something moved—was it a cat? No, it was a boy! A pair of blue eyes looked at him through the leaves.

'Hallo,' said Alexander, pleased. 'Are you from next door?'

The boy crawled through the undergrowth and stood up. He was wearing green trousers, a green shirt, a battered green felt hat that was too big for his head and he was holding a home-made bow and a bunch of arrows.

Alexander and the boy stared at each other with interest. Then the boy spoke.

'I live next door. I didn't know there were any kids living here.'

'I'm just here for a holiday,' explained Alexander. 'Are you Willy?'

The boy pulled a face. 'No! I'm William Tell.'

'You're joking!'

'I'm not joking,' said William Tell. 'It's my real name.'

Alexander grinned. 'And I'm Alexander the Great!'

William snorted, 'Now *you're* joking!'

'Well,' said Alexander, 'Alexander Jones, actually.'

William changed the subject. 'Can't you walk?'

'No,' said Alexander.

William sighed. 'Just my luck—I was hoping to

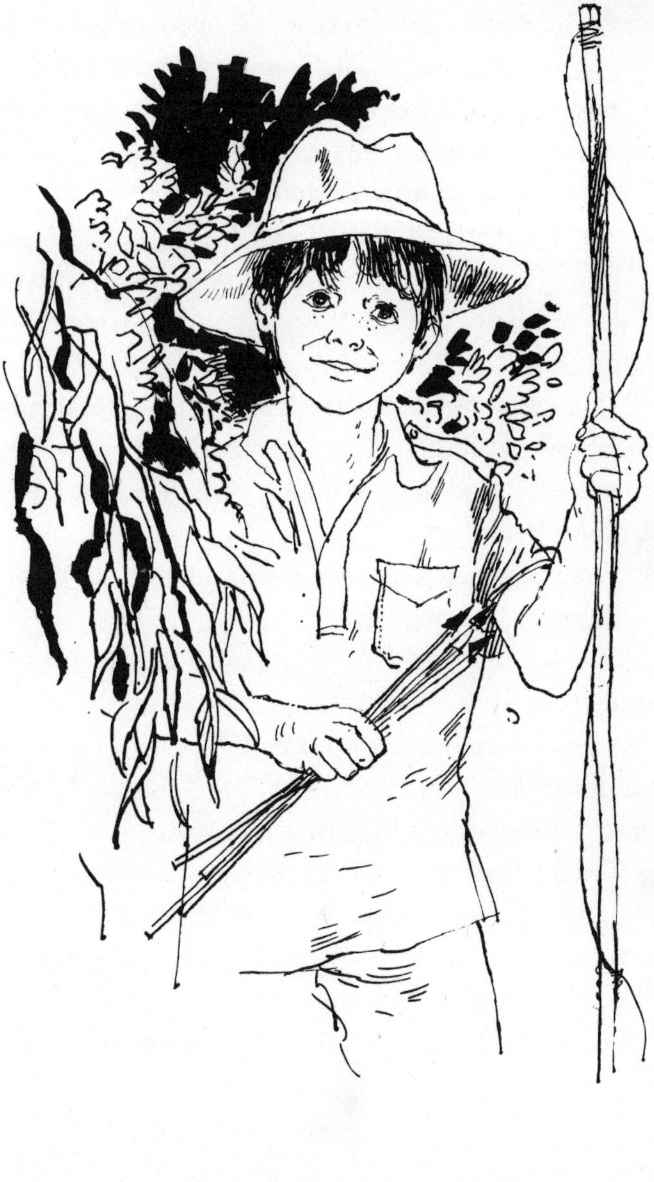

play William Tell with someone. We learned about him at school before the holidays. He refused to bow to Gessler's hat and had to shoot an apple off his son's head. It's really exciting—jumping out of the boat in a storm, escaping from the soldiers, saving Switzerland and all that.'

Alexander laughed. 'I knew your name wasn't really William Tell. Anyway, you look more like Robin Hood in those clothes!'

William looked a bit deflated. 'I reckon he probably would have worn things like this, too,' he shrugged. 'And if you must know, my name is William Bell.'

Alexander was sorry for laughing at him. 'Okay, William Tell—what shall we do?'

William frowned. 'Well, we can't run around or hide in bushes or anything. But how about me shooting an apple off your head?'

Alexander was alarmed. 'No, thanks! How about shooting some off that tree instead?'

William looked at the apple tree. 'That's a good idea,' he agreed. 'It's loaded with apples. Well, you first—only you know William Tell really had a crossbow, not one like this.'

Alexander took the bow with a thrill of excitement. 'I've never used a bow before,' he confessed.

William came behind his wheelchair, and leant over to explain how to hold the arrow and where to put his fingers on the bow. After a bit of fumbling, Alexander tried a shot. It took a lot more attempts to do it properly. At first the arrow just plopped onto the ground in front of him. Once he got really muddled up and somehow threw the bow instead of the arrow. William rolled on the grass laughing until Alexander wished he could kick him. At last he managed to shoot as far as the tree. William took over then, and Alexander watched admiringly as he hit one apple after another. 'Hey, you are really good!'

William grinned. 'This tree's so crowded with apples it's hard to miss!' He counted the apples. 'That's six hits out of ten shots. Now you have ten shots.'

He put the apples in a little pile and handed the bow over. Alexander tried very hard, but he hit only two apples. Then it was William's turn again. He aimed carefully, and scored eight. Alexander was determined to do better and he became very serious as he fitted the arrows to the bow. He shot off ten arrows without saying a single word—and amazingly he managed to score six! He let out a whoop. 'Hooray!' he yelled, while William flung himself back on the grass in a mock faint.

A voice called through the bushes. 'What on earth are you shouting about?' It was Alexander's aunt.

William looked stricken. 'I'm going!' he muttered, scrambling to his feet.

Alexander grabbed the back of his shirt. 'Oh, no, you're not!'

Aunt Rosemary came up the path. 'I'm glad to see you've found a friend, Alexander,' she said. 'I suppose this is Willy from next door?'

Alexander felt too guilty to say anything, so he just nodded. William was looking very embarrassed.

'I won't eat you,' said Aunt Rosemary. 'Don't look so uncomfortable. What have you been playing—ah, bows and arrows!'

Alexander couldn't understand why she wasn't cross. Surely she had seen the ruined apples all over the grass?

'Have you been teaching Alexander?' she asked William, who was trying not to squirm. 'That's something I've often meant to do myself. I used to be quite good at archery when I was young.' She pointed to the topmost branch of the apple tree. 'See that apple, that little one up there?'

Alexander and William stared at Aunt Rosemary in amazement as she picked up the bow and arrow and took aim. Twang—squish! Two halves of the apple fell to the ground.

'Still a good shot,' she said simply. 'Not a bad bow, Willy.'

The boys were still wondering what to make of it all when Aunt Rosemary handed the bow back to William and laughed. 'And now, you horrible little brats, pick up all my poor apples and come down to the kitchen to be punished!'

The two watched her disappear down the path, looked at each other and shrugged. When they got to the kitchen, laden with apples, Aunt Rosemary was waiting. She handed them vegetable peelers and knives, saying, 'Wash your hands and set to work.'

Alexander and William spent the rest of the morning peeling and slicing apples. They had never done it before and it was not easy. It was so fiddly and boring, and their fingers got cramped and sticky. They hated it! Aunt Rosemary came in to do

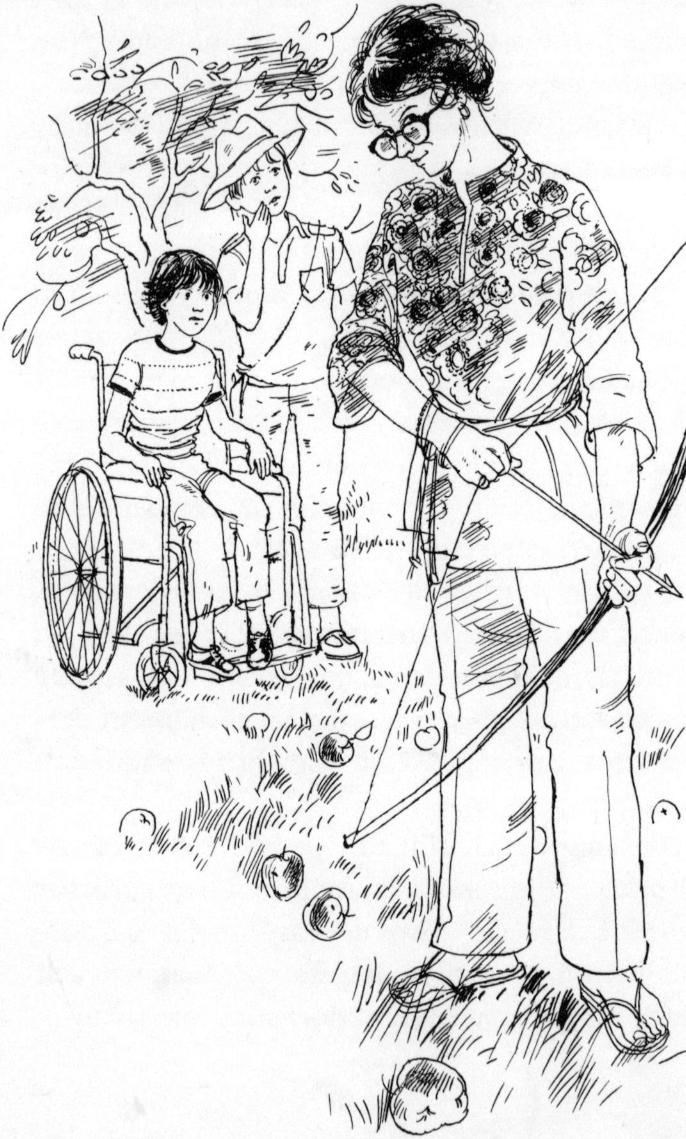

some baking just as they finished. They washed their aching hands and thankfully handed over the huge bowl of apple pieces for approval. Aunt Rosemary looked at the hacked about pieces of apple and gave a little smile. 'Serves you right,' she said.

After William had been sent home with the proof of his wickedness in the form of a delicious apple pie, Alexander and his aunt sat down to lunch. Alexander had just decided that, after all, it had been a pretty fair punishment when Aunt Rosemary spoke.

'I think,' she said sternly, 'I will have to speak to Uncle Bernard about this business.'

Alexander nearly choked on a mouthful of apple crumble, but Aunt Rosemary was firm. She did speak to Uncle Bernard, who looked very solemn and disappeared into his garage for a long time.

The next morning, when Alexander went out, he met William in the garden leaping about excitedly.

'Hey—your uncle's just great! Look what he gave me this morning. Now we can practise properly.'

Alexander stared. Propped up against a nearby bush was a freshly painted target board. Terrific!

But wasn't something a little strange? The bullseye was painted not red but green.

Alexander peered closer, and then began to laugh.

'It's not a bullseye at all. It's an apple!'

Alexander in the Bath

Alexander had spent all week making wooden boats and he wanted to try them out in the bath.

'I'm sorry, but I haven't time to run a bath specially for your boats,' his mother said on Saturday morning. 'Use the basin.'

'But it's not big enough,' protested Alexander.

'Well, I'm afraid you'll just have to wait until I get back,' answered Mrs Jones, rummaging on the telephone table. 'Oh, where are the car keys? I promised to meet Aunt Rosemary in town at ten o'clock and I'm so late.'

Alexander looked under the telephone. 'Here they are.'

'Who put them there?' wondered Mrs Jones. 'Never mind—I had better go. I'll be back at lunch time, so please try to keep out of trouble till then!'

Alexander listened until he heard his mother's car drive away. He had waited all week to try those boats, and now he was determined to do so. He put his boats carefully on the shelf beside the bath and wondered how on earth he was going to put in the plug. He looked round the bathroom for inspiration, and finally decided that he could push it in. He unhooked the big wooden back-scrubber from the back of the door. Then he dropped the plug into the bath and gently nudged it with the long handle towards the hole.

'Ah, that's it,' he said as he tapped the plug firmly into place. 'Now for the water.' Alexander stretched out as far as he dared over the bath. 'Bother, I can't reach the tap. Now what shall I do?' He thought hard for a minute. 'I know. I'll try pushing it on with the back-scrubber!'

Feeling very pleased with himself, Alexander leaned over and poked at the tap handle. A few hard prods with the back-scrubber and the tap came on.

Alexander waited for the water to rise. As soon as the level was high enough for him to reach, he leaned over to turn off the tap, but then he realised he was in trouble.

'I turned the tap on by pushing the handle away from me, which means I have to *pull* the handle to turn it off. But that's impossible. I can't get a grip on it. There's no way I can pull the handle towards me!'

Alexander stared in growing horror as the water

continued to rise, and he tried not to panic as more and more water flowed into the bath. He must do something quickly before it overflowed onto the floor and then flooded the whole house!

'If I can't turn the tap off, perhaps I can pull out the plug?' he thought desperately. 'But the only way I can reach to pull out the plug is to get into the bath!'

Alexander was so anxious by now that he didn't stop to think any further. He turned his chair to face the bath, brought it up as close as possible, and put the brake on. The water was rising so steadily there was no time to pull off his shoes. Quickly he lifted his legs one by one into the bath. He held firmly to the seat of the chair and hoisted himself onto the edge of the bath. 'Perhaps I can reach the tap from here,' he thought.

He stretched forwards towards the tap, slipped and fell face first into the water, banging his elbow on the way. The water rushed over the edge and onto the floor. Alexander pushed himself up for air, gasping. The water was freezing! He grabbed the tap and turned it hard, once, twice, and a third time. At last the water stopped. The next thing was to let out some of the water, but the bath was so full that

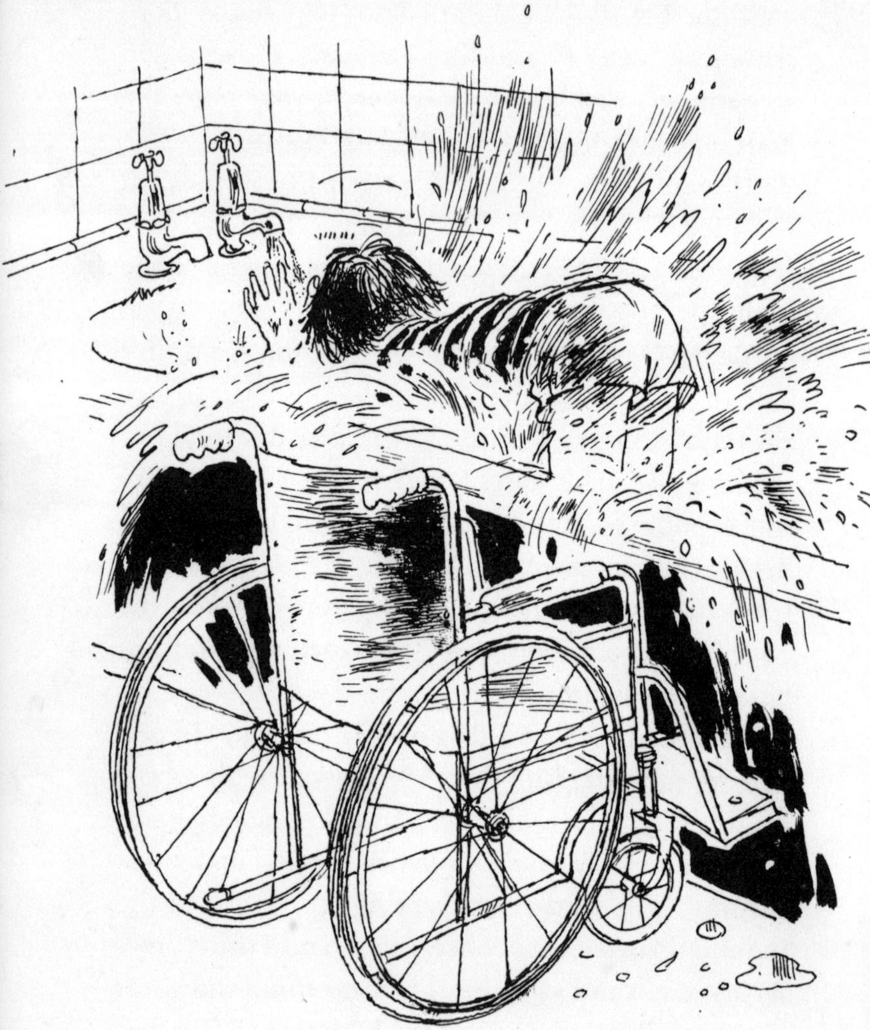

the plug was jammed tightly in the drain. Alexander struggled with that plug until he felt his fingers were turning into frozen spaghetti. He was very cold, and his arms were tired with the efforts of holding his head out of the water. He tugged at the plug, he jiggled it, he yanked it and he twisted it, and at last it came free. 'Thank goodness!' he panted. He dropped the plug over the edge of the bath and watched the water go down. It seemed to take ages at first, and his clothes tickled him as the water level went down. For the last few inches it speeded up a bit, and finally, with a loud slurp and gurgle, the remaining stream glugged down the drain.

Alexander was very relieved to see it go, but now he had other problems. He was face down in the bath with all his clothes on, including his shoes and socks, he was soaking wet and he had no way of getting out.

Alexander wriggled over on to his back and pulled himself up. Now that he was sitting up he could at least take off his soggy clothes. He untied his water-logged shoes and pulled off his sopping socks and dropped them onto the floor. Squdge! Then he tugged off his soaked T-shirt and squeezed the water out of it in a half-hearted way. He dropped it overboard as well. Splop! He knew it would be a struggle to get his shorts off, so he left them on. Goose-pimples prickled up all over his body.

'Brr!' he shivered. 'If only I could reach a towel.' He rubbed his arms and looked round the room. The towels were way out of reach, but the bathmat wasn't. It was on the shelf at the end of the bath where he had put his boats.

'And I didn't even get a chance to try them out,' he muttered gloomily as he picked up the bathmat. It was a bit prickly, and rather sandy as well, but it was better than nothing, so he wrapped it around his cold shoulders. He sat sadly in the bath in a little puddle of water and wondered how long it would be before his mother came home. He was just beginning to feel very sorry for himself, when he heard someone calling from outside.

'Hey! Is anyone home?'

With a big rush of thankfulness, Alexander yelled as loudly as he possibly could, 'LUCY! HELP!'

He heard the front door flung open and footsteps racing down the hall.

'Alexander,' called Lucy in a fright. 'Are you all right? Where are you?'

'In the bathroom!' he shouted.

Lucy burst in and stopped dead. Alexander stared at her white face.

'I'm sorry, Lucy. I didn't mean to frighten you.'

Lucy leant against the wall and said weakly, 'You beast, Alexander. I thought you were dying or something!' Then she looked at all the water on the floor. 'And just what are you doing? Why are you sitting in the bath wearing a bathmat?'

'Just help me out and I'll explain.'

'But I can't get you out by myself, you idiot! You're much too heavy!'

Alexander brightened up. 'I know, phone Tony and ask him to help. He's got a bike, so it won't take him long to get over here.'

'Okay,' agreed Lucy and she disappeared through the door. Alexander felt silly sitting in the bath while Lucy used the telephone, but luckily Tony was at home, and it wasn't long before he came pedalling round to the rescue. Together he and Lucy took hold of Alexander and began to lift him out.

'You're getting fat,' groaned Tony.

Lucy giggled and nearly dropped Alexander back in the bath, but at last he was safely in his chair.

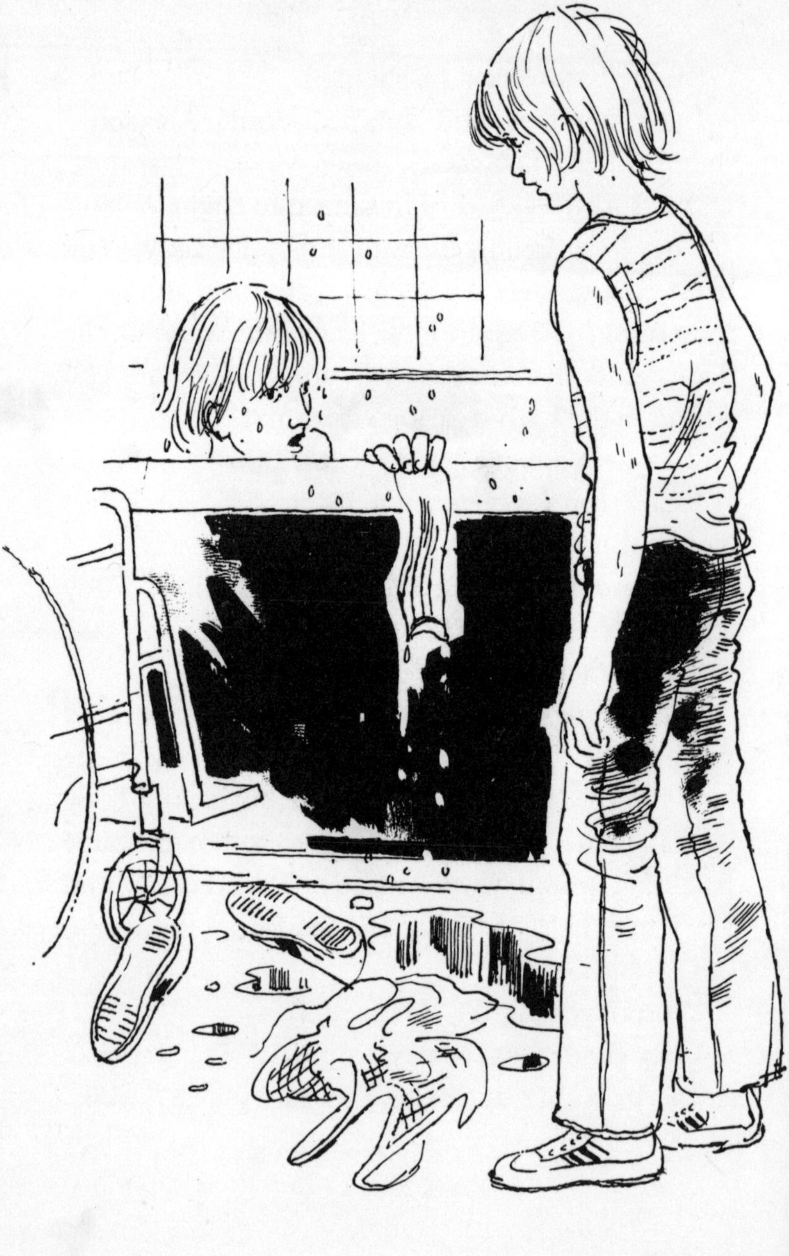

Tony went with him to the bedroom and helped him into some dry clothes.

'I've mopped up the water on the bathroom floor,' announced Lucy smugly, as she came in. 'Aren't I good? *And* I've hung your wet things on the clothes line.'

Just as Alexander opened his mouth to thank her, his mother walked in at the door. The children looked at each other, and Mrs Jones instantly saw three guilty faces. 'Oh, no!' she said. 'What has he been doing now?'

Alexander looked pleadingly at the others, as if to say, 'Don't go!' Then he took a deep breath and told his mother all about it.

Mrs Jones looked cross. 'It was very stupid of you to get into the bath. You could easily have drowned.'

Alexander privately agreed with her, remembering the awful moment when he had fallen in. 'It would have been all right, if I could have turned off the tap,' he said hopefully.

'You should think things through first,' reminded Mrs Jones. She went to the bathroom. 'Come here, all three of you,' she called.

Alexander, Lucy and Tony crowded in. Mrs

Jones pushed the tap on with the back-scrubber. 'This is how you turned it on—right?'

Alexander nodded. Mrs Jones continued, 'Now watch this.'

She pushed the tap the other way, once, twice and again. The water slowed down to a trickle and stopped, except for a few drips. 'You didn't need to pull the handle at all, Alexander. All you had to do was to push it in the opposite direction!' She smiled at his red face. 'You do like to do things the hard way.'

Tony and Lucy burst out laughing, and after a minute Alexander grinned as well. 'What a nut,' he agreed sheepishly.

Mrs Jones gave Lucy a hug and ruffled Tony's hair. 'Thanks for helping this dunce out of trouble,' she said. 'How about staying for lunch? I've brought a terrific cake back from town.'

The cake *was* terrific. Mrs Jones cut large creamy slices, but she didn't have any herself. 'I'll only get fat,' she said wistfully. 'Anyway, while you eat yours I'll just pop up to the hardware shop for a minute.'

She was back before the cake was completely eaten so she was able to rescue the remains for tea.

'What did you buy?' asked Alexander.

Mrs Jones smiled and produced a long thin chain with a ring on one end and a hook on the other. She showed it to Alexander. 'The ring goes over the tap handle, my boy, and the other end hooks onto the bath plug. So when you want to let out the water you just have to pull up the chain!'

Alexander wriggled uncomfortably. 'You know I won't do it again, Mum.'

'That's what you say,' joked Tony.

Lucy was remembering how heavy Alexander was to haul out of the bathtub. 'I think it's a great idea!' she said.